Melodies Of A Broken Vase

A Journey Through Shattered Echoes

Kajolee Rahate

Made with ❤ on the BookLeaf Publishing Platform
www.bookleafpub.in
www.bookleafpub.com

Dedication

"To the ones who loved even when it hurt, who kept believing in empathy and kindness when the world gave them every reason not to. To the wandering souls who gather their broken pieces and turn them into poetry, and to the dreamers who find music in their own shattering—this book is for you. May you know that even a broken vase can still hold light, and even the softest melody can heal a weary heart."

Preface

Poetry has always held a special place in my heart. Since I was eleven, it has been my refuge—words stitched together like fragile laces, holding the fragments of emotions too vast to contain. Melodies of a Broken Vase is not just a collection of poems; it is a journey through the echoes of love, loss, healing, and hope.

Each piece within these pages carries a small part of me —a whisper of moments lived and feelings that demanded to be written. Some poems are quiet, like the wind brushing against an open window; others are storms that rage through the soul. Yet, they all sing the same truth: that even broken things can hold beauty, that even shattered echoes can create music.

This book is for those who have felt too deeply, for the ones who have loved and lost, and for those searching for meaning in the in-betweens of life. I hope these words find you where you are—and remind you that even in brokenness, there is art. Even in grief, there is beauty.

With all my heart and soul,

Kajolee Rahate

Acknowledgements

*In the quietest corners of my heart, this book was born—
a collection of fragments, some shattered, others whole,
yet each piece a part of the journey that brought me
here. Melodies of a Broken Vase is not just a reflection of
brokenness, but of the resilience that blooms even in the
most fractured places.*

*First, I must thank the quiet voices that have guided me
through moments of darkness and light, those who stood
by me without asking for anything in return. To the
parents who patiently listened to my thoughts, the silent
supporters who believed in me even when I doubted
myself, and to my sister, whose unwavering support was
the warmth in my coldest hours, thank you for being my
foundation when I felt lost. Your presence gave me the
strength to write, to create, and to heal.*

*To my friends , whose love has always been my quiet
strength, thank you for nurturing me in ways I will
never fully comprehend. Your faith in me helped me hold
my pen steady through every tear and every moment of
doubt.*

*A special thank you to the countless souls whose stories,
dreams, and struggles have unknowingly woven their
way into the fabric of these poems. You have been my
muses in ways you will never know. And to those who*

walked beside me during my most challenging days,
your presence has been the ink in my words.
Finally, to the silent moments when words felt
impossible, thank you for teaching me that even silence
has a song—one that can be broken and still beautiful.
This book is for you.

THE ECHO IN HER SILENCE

She was a warrior, built to endure,
Yet no one had warned her that pain had no cure.
She fought through the silence, she bled through the
night,
But battles unspoken don't end in the light.

She carried her sorrow like whispers of rain,
Drowning, yet smiling, in love with her pain.
Her voice was a shadow, her tears left unseen,
A ghost in the mirror of who she had been.

How could she not shatter from all she had lost?
The weight of their words, the lines she had crossed?
She held out her hands but found only air,
For love isn't love when no one is there.

She stitched up her wounds with the threads of her past,
But seams come undone when they're mended too fast.
She wanted to trust, to hope, to believe,

Yet nothing had stayed—no promise, no dream.

So she learned to stand when her legs gave way,
To silence the echoes that begged her to stay.
She burned every name that had carved through her
skin,
And rose from the ashes, her own to begin.

They made their vows, they swore, they lied,
But she'd had enough of love that died.
So she tied herself to her own soul,
For no one stays only she was her whole.

THE LIBRARY OF HER SOUL

She holds a library deep inside,
With shelves where ghostly stories hide.
Each page she inks, each soul she keeps,
Tucked away where silence sleeps.

She's written tales a thousandfold,
Of fleeting warmth and hands gone cold.
Yet some she burned, the flames ran too high,
For words too stained, for love that has died.

She's named each book for what she's felt,
Like oceans where lost dreams have dwelt.
A nursery, too, she's sown with care—
A garden of faces once resting there.

Her ink replaced her blood one night,
She writes in sorrow, black and white.
But one book haunts her, feared the most—
"Broken Trust and Fading Hope."

She never wished to pen that tale,
Yet chapter by chapter, it set sail.
A list of names in sorrow's hue,
Each wound exposed, each scar in view.

And so she built her walls up high,
No key, no door, no open sky.
For every time she let one in,
They carved her soul and left again.

Yet still, she waits for one so bold,
Who'd climb the cliffs through winds so cold.
Who'd dive into her endless sea,
And close that book eternally.

Who'd set her mind in burning light,
Yet keep her heart both fierce and bright.
Who'd take her ink and let it flow,
Not for the past—but tales unknown.

For she is tired of writing pain,
Of hearts that left, of love in vain.
She longs for hands to pull her through—
For someone who would change her,
And the stories too.

THE GIRL WHO LIVED

Let me tell you an enchanting story,
Of a girl who bore her scars with glory.
She braved the seas, the raging tide,
Through storms that tried to break her stride.

She wandered deserts, vast and wide,
Where stolen dreams and whispers lied.
She walked through fire, she faced the cold,
Yet in her heart, she never sold.

She climbed the cliffs, the jagged height,
And dove where depths consumed the light.
And even as the waters pulled,
She fought, she rose, she took control.

She smiled at flowers and danced in rain,
Yet wept when memories brought her pain.
The sun would glow to greet her face,
The moon would mourn in its embrace.

Through silent nights, the shadows wept,
Their silver tears in dawn were kept.
She feared not death, nor ghosts unseen,
But hearts that hurt and souls unclean.

She gazed upon her shattered home,
Where winter winds still softly moan.
She could not mend the broken past,
And so she wept as it did not last.

Yet still she loves, and still she's loved,
A spirit fierce, yet free as doves.
For time, though cruel, could not conceal,
The fire within she will always yield.

THE SACRED HOARD

You are not a fabled being,
Not a warrior crowned in lore.
You do not wear a vampire's grin,
Nor rule lands with sword or roar.

You've wasted hours chasing shadows,
Nights dissolving into dreams,
Believing you belonged to them—
That fate would mend the seams.

But no, this is not their kingdom.
You were never just a pawn.
Human or not, you were chosen—
To rise before the dawn.

So wake from sleep, O wandering soul,
The veil has thinned at last.
The world you see now shakes and burns—
It echoes of your past.

What you are is not your sin,
What you're not may still unfold.
The truth you seek, the fire you fear,
Lies in the heart you hold.

We may need you yet, brave one—
To lift the blade concealed,
The one that rests beneath your grief,
In ruins unrevealed.

Ransack your fears and tear them down,
Let go of all you've known.
For buried deep inside your chest,
A sacred flame has grown.

THE HIGH PRICE

If you fear the thorns you see,
You have no right to touch the rose—
O dolent soul, do you not know
What pain such beauty bestows?

As water turns to dew upon her petals,
And a lush red glow begins to gleam,
You gaze with an intoxicated longing,
Tempted by a velvet dream.

A little closer still you move,
Unable to let such purity go.
You reach to feel her silken grace—
A touch so soft, your fingers glow.

A wave of heat, a thrill, a rush,
As you mingle with her bloom,
You bring your hand down gently now,
Unaware you approach your doom.

The poison waits, concealed in charm,
It pricks your skin—so sharp, unseen.
Your smile falters, your lips grow pale,
You grasp at air, lost in between.

You cannot move.
You cannot cry.
And in that final breath,
You surely know—you won't survive.

THE HORIZON ARC

I've parted ways with shadows that once pulled me
down,
With voices that saw me only as someone bound to
drown.
I've walked away from wars, from bloodshed and the
cries,
From the ghosts of the fallen, with hollow, staring eyes.

I've come a long way from the ruins man designed,
Searching for the fracture that still haunts this time.
I've returned to reignite the flame that pierced the dark,
To carry light across the curve of the horizon's arc.

I survived the war that shattered all and none,
Praised kings whose crowns weighed heavy but did
nothing once won.
I was melody in the symphony the gods had sung,
And oracle to seekers, their questions always young.

I've been many things, yet always just one—

Never merely human, never easily undone.
Love never burdened me with soft and fragile care,
For now the world is harsher, and peace is rare.

They say love makes you weak—
A shimmer on the surface of waters far too deep.
But I found strength in every hue it brings,
A wild, wondrous force with a thousand wings.

I've learned not to fight for what poisons the soul,
Even evil once held good—once played its role.
So I'll cleanse the stains of war from every path I take,
Reach near and far for hearts I might wake.

I'll build a world more worthy than the last,
For I've seen its end, and lived through its past.
And I will rise for what must still be done,
To be the voice, the light, the holy one.

THE GIFT OF WANDERING

I read a book once—
About travelers, wanderers, and souls ablaze,
With fire in their eyes and kaleidoscopes in their gaze.
People who believe in living wide and deep,
Who chase their dreams while the rest of us sleep.

They give their all to every quest,
To places untouched, where wild hearts rest.
Far from the noise of a crowded land,
They search for worlds not built by man's hand.

To see the sun at its brightest height,
To dance with wolves, to bathe in moonlight.
To chirp with birds and dive with fish,
To live each day as a silent wish.

Among creatures who don't know greed,
Where nothing hurts, and no one bleeds.
They seek caves that whisper myths untold,
Doorways to realms of harmony and gold.

A world where every life is worth,
Where sorrow holds no claim on Earth.
Where sunlight wraps you in warm embrace,
And darkness hums a lullaby's grace.

Where unpredictability brings no fear,
And joy echoes loud, crystal clear.
Like a gift wrapped in cherry-red silk and gold,
More beautiful than stories ever told.

And when they find it, in the end,
It isn't a place—it's a person, a friend.
It's love that feels like endless skies,
Or a haven where no one wears disguise.

That is the magic of those who roam—
They aren't just searching for land,
They're searching for a home.

DESTINED

They told her—
"You were born for greater things."
Yet sorrow came on silent wings.

Before her courage found its name,
Pity wrapped her heart in shame.

In halls adorned by hollow grace,
She wore a smile to mask her place.

With quiet strength she bore the weight,
Of love denied and twisted fate.

She dared to dream, to disobey,
But hid her fire far away.

No soul could reach her secret core,
Not even when she won the war.

She chose to hide her pain from view,

To rise in silence, fierce and true.

Refusing pity, praise, or plea—
She bore her truth with dignity.

Her madness sleeps beneath the veil,
Her power wrapped in moonlight pale.

Enchanted woods may come and go,
But she has seen their ebb and flow.

One day her light will touch the sky,
But none will see her soaring high.

She walks unknown, yet never lost—
A soul that learned to bear the cost.

TO RISE

Lifting up to serve,
Yet growing just to be looked down upon—
Safe places exist no more,
The secured castles are gone.

Out in the world, you come to see
Exactly how harsh life can be.
Mistakes are made, and lessons learned,
From each belief, a truth discerned.

Sustainability feels like a dream,
Until you've lost your final gleam.
With empty hands, you're forced to ask—
Where will you stand when stripped of your mask?

So grow—not just tall, but wise.
Grow to soar above the skies.
Grow to reach your truest heights,
Grow to win your quiet fights.

Learn from all—both young and old,
Let your heart be brave and bold.
Hate no soul, love everyone,
And leave your mark before you're done.

THE FATEFUL HUES

I wish I could hold myself close,
While the world stayed far away—
I wish the boulders weren't this heavy,
Crushing me deeper every day.

I wish the horizon weren't so far,
I'm tired of chasing lines that flee,
Or maybe I'm just tired of,
Wondering if it's meant for me.

I'm squeezing through a faceless crowd,
Strangers rushing past the night,
Trying to reach somewhere unknown,
Before the dawn breaks cold and white.

My fingers might freeze, my legs might give,
My courage fade, my magic fall—
Because maybe I'm too scared to crawl,
Yet we all start small, after all.

I forgot the steps before the stride,
I forgot what roots the rise—
And now I see I've walked askew,
Chasing echoes, chasing lies.

Perhaps I've ridden the wrong horse,
Galloped toward a borrowed fate—
But I won't surrender, not just yet,
There's still a door beyond this gate.

The sapphire isn't always blue,
Sometimes it burns in emerald hue—
Look close, you'll find it shifting too—
A thousand truths in every view.

THE PATH OF BECOMING

I would throw caution to the wind,
My prowess still unknown,
A quiet force of equanimity,
With roots now overgrown.

Once a proponent of perfect grace,
A pedantic soul beneath the sun,
Born from struggle, bred by fire,
Always fleeing, always on the run.

I sniffed the air like wild perfume,
Hoping to find my kind,
Feasting on pride and bitter stems,
Leaving old selves behind.

Lost in habits, hobbling on,
A prodigy turned to myth,
Damaged by the touch of fools,
Yet I still exist.

Survived it all—every storm,
Each necessity a guide,
Though hope ran thin, I held on tight,
With no one at my side.

I lost my sight but not my soul,
No stranger filled my place,
I found my fire, my deep desire,
And walked the path with grace.

THE GLOOM THAT HELD ON

Every day, the skies turn gray,
As if the clouds will break and sway—
To shed their tears in thunder's song,
To pour it out, to right the wrong.

But each time, they hold it in,
Swallowing storms that churn within.

Just like us, they bear the strain,
And wear a smile through silent rain.

They teach us strength in subtle ways,
In quiet nights and heavy days.

You might be trembling on a ledge,
A breath away from slipping edge,
Yet still, you hold, you do not fall,
You brave the dark, you face it all.

And that's what life is truly about—
Not roaring flames, but gentle doubt.
To bend, not break, through storms above,
To carry on—because you love.

AT THE EDGE OF DAWN

At dawn, she'd hum her favorite tune,
Bathed in the light of a fading moon.
In her backyard, wild and wide,
With forest green on every side.

The mountains bowed to hear her voice,
A melody that made the air rejoice.
Each note that drifted from her soul,
Made her wonder if this was what it meant to be whole.

She'd swirl and twirl with barefoot grace,
As leaves rained gently on her face.
Like confetti they'd fall, in quiet delight;
Dancing with her in morning's light.

As the sky turned from gold to blue,
The cricket would join with a song or two.
And when the day began to rise,
She'd step away from open skies.

Back to her window, dark and still,
With dreams that only dawn could fill.
She'd wait again for morning's bloom,
To sing once more and chase the gloom.

I DON'T WANT TO BE A BROKEN VASE

I don't want to be a broken vase—
Belittled, bruised, a scattered case,
Shards of silence on the floor,
A relic no one fights for anymore.

I don't want to be a fractured frame,
Held responsible for all the blame,
For fate's foul hand or twisted thread,
For dreams now dust, and words unsaid.

I don't want to be splintered glass,
Too sharp to touch, too weak to last,
Too weary to piece what time undid,
Too tired to search for what hope hid.

I don't want to be a fading mark,
A voiceless echo in the dark,
Diminished by a daily sting,
An insect crushed beneath a wing.

I don't want their soft despair,
Their pity cloaked in practiced care—
Let them see the flame I bore,
Not the cracks I won't restore.

I don't want to be cliché grief,
A tale too common, too brief—
A broken vase the world can read,
But never feel, nor truly heed.

THE GAME YOU THOUGHT YOU WON

No, tell me—
Do you love diamonds,
Or the enchantment they disguise?
Are you drawn to decadent delights,
Because fewer taste what wealth can buy?
Do you crave the costly feast,
Knowing others starve beneath your sky?

Do you play golf for the joy it brings,
Or just to look sharp in designer things?
While inside, your soul is caving in,
Like a coaster that's lost its tracks in the wind.
You call on God in a desperate cry,
But even He won't meet your eye.

You thought riches gave you reign,
A throne above the common strain—
But now your hands, too small, too bare,
Can't carry the weight you chose to wear.

You own the world, yet can't command,
The trembling of your weakened hands.

You lost the game you thought you'd won,
A castle built beneath no sun.
And when truth came, it didn't knock—
It shattered glass and stopped the clock.
What good are crowns if you die alone,
Surrounded by gold, but carved in stone?

I WAS NEVER MEANT TO STAY

I was never a keeper—
And deep down, I knew it.
Like the storm-chasing wind,
I'd arrive... then outgrew it.

I was freedom in motion,
Not obedient, nor tame,
A wildfire of mistakes—
Each one carved my name.

I never paused, not even once,
No moment held me tight.
And people stared, confused and torn,
By someone born of flight.

I was never made for stillness,
Nor quiet, nor refrain—
I was that scent of sugar toast
That flickers down the lane.

I was the aftertaste of night,
That fades with morning's glow.
I was the letter to your mom—
The ache you never show.

I was the fog on silver dawns,
That melts with rays of sun,
The bloom that wilts too early,
The stream too cold to run.

I'd slip beneath your blanket's crease,
Like air so sharp and shy,
But I won't stay for summer's heat,
I was never meant to try.

For I am made of leaving,
Of whispers, and of sighs,
Of things that pass and linger on—
In heartbeats and goodbyes.

So don't try to hold me, darling,
I'm not a thing to own.
I'll be there—yes, truly be there—
But I'll never be your home.

IN THE SHATTERS OF HUMANITY

In the shatters of humanity,
Did you dwell in a house of stone—
Or roam the ruins restlessly,
Mending broken hearts alone?
Did you wrestle with your enemies
With painted nails and grace,
Or were you forced to draw your blades
In that cruel and hopeless place?
Did you laugh when the sword struck deep,
Brave through every scar—
Or crumble when the pain outgrew
What you believed you are?
Did their ruthless lies unravel
All the faith you held inside,
Or teach you, through the aching truth,
That trust and time collide?
Did you survive the silent war
Within cold concrete walls—
Or rise again on trembling legs,

Unafraid of future falls?
I hope you forged a reason to live,
When the world offered none,
That your courage burned a brighter fire
Than the dark could ever shun.
I hope you find a will to fight—
A flame that does not fall—
For the soul who won't take up their sword,
May never rise at all.

CRUMBLES

The crumbs of childhood scattered wide,
Blown far along the winds of time,
And when we step in lands unknown,
We spot those traces, soft with grime.

We reach for them with open hands—
So worn, yet oddly sweet—
Forgetting we once cast them off,
To find a life complete.

We gather them, then build a home
That feels both old and right,
But stitch in pain from days gone by
While calling it delight.

We let old shadows in again,
Believing they belong,
Not knowing we invite the hurt
We've carried all along.

And so our past begins to breathe
Within the walls we mend—
A bittersweet reminder that
Some cycles never really end.

OCEAN BLUES

They call me calm as the ocean wide,
But they don't see the storm I hide—
The rage that coils beneath the blue,
The pain that tides and surges through.

They praise the peace upon my face,
Unknowing of the war I chase.
Each wave that sways with tender grace
Has buried screams it can't erase.

They do not hear the silent toll
Of battles fought to save my soul,
Nor count the wreckage lost to time—
The sunken dreams, the silent crime.

Oh, they don't know the numbered dead,
The hopes that drowned, the words unsaid.
For every calm that meets the eye,
There's thunder echoing in the sky.

It was not fate that brought me here,
Not luck, nor chance, nor freedom clear.
But scars I earned with every breath—
My triumphs carved from trials and death.

So call me calm, but know this too:
This peace was fought for, hard and true.
And though I swell with silent grace,
A storm still stirs beneath my face.

THE WITHERING

There was a summer breeze calling my name,
Like a fragile butterfly, I soared in its flame,
I flew, far, far away,
Chasing the whispers that led me astray.

They yearned for me to spread the word,
To share the wonders that I'd observed,
A world so remarkable, a treasure so pure,
A dream I had nurtured, a light to endure.

But when I reached the edge of my quest,
The winter came, and stole my rest,
It swept away every gleam of light,
And left me cold, alone in the night.

The warmth I longed to give the world,
Fell silent, a flicker that swirled,
I couldn't transmit the fire within,
So I gathered the frost, let it begin.

I hoarded the cold, let it take its toll,
Until my heart froze, and took its soul.
My body crumbled with each passing day,
Until the chill took all warmth away.

By the time I returned to that summer breeze,
I was hollow, lost, longing for ease.
The warmth I once knew, the joy I held tight,
Faded to shadows, lost in the night.

I could not feel the sun's soft kiss,
Nor find the happiness I once missed.
For in my flight, I left my heart,
And now, the magic is torn apart.

I'M NOT BURNED OUT YET

I'm not burned out yet,
The fire in my eyes still gleams,
Untouched, intact,
Even though my body's gone cold.

Like a Venus flytrap,
My hands remain soft, still warm,
I'm not burned out yet,
Though I've shattered the hopes of my passionate self,
I've hidden some away, deep inside.

One day—
One fine day—I'll let it all out,
I'm not burned out yet.
I have a list of people and places,
Stored low in my brain,
Poems flushed in the toilet,
Still etched in my mind.

Ready to spread,
As soon as I release them,
As soon as I allow them,
I'm not burned out yet.
I've forgiven the sins of many,
But my eyes still scorch.

There's still fire,
Enough to set ablaze the unbroken forest,
Reducing it to dust and ash.
I'm not burned out yet,
I'm still alive, at peace,
With myself and the world.

Ready to conquer,
Ready to relive every dream—
Destroy, but never deceive.